THE CHEMICAL LIFE

The Chemical Life

JIM JOHNSTONE

THE POETRY IMPRINT AT VÉHICULE PRESS

Published with the generous assistance of The Canada Council for the Arts and the Canada Book Fund of the Department of Canadian Heritage, Government of Canada.

Funded by the Government of Canada
Financé par le gouvernement du Canada
Canada

Signal Editions Editor: Carmine Starnino

Cover design: David Drummond
Photo of the author: Erica Smith
Set in Filosofia and Minion by Simon Garamond
Printed by Marquis Book Printing Inc.

Dépôt légal, Library and Archives Canada and the Bibliothèque national du Québec, third trimester 2017.

Library and Archives Canada Cataloguing in Publication

Johnstone, Jim, 1978-, author
The chemical life / Jim Johnstone.

Poems.
Issued in print and electronic formats.
ISBN 978-1-55065-482-0 (softcover)

I. Title.

PS8619.O489.C44 2017 C811'.6 C2017-903134-1

Published by Véhicule Press, Montréal, Québec, Canada
www.vehiculepress.com

Distribution in Canada by LitDistCo
www.litdistco.ca

Distribution in the U.S. by Independent Publishers Group
www.ipgbook.com

Printed in Canada on FSC ® certified paper.

for Liberty Village

CONTENTS

For the others, like me, there is only the flash
Of negative knowledge, the night when, drunk, one
Staggers to the bathroom and stares in the glass
To meet one's madness

—W.H. AUDEN

The Chemical Life

I unzip and adjust
the screen—
a second skyline
rises over the keys,

my likeness tilted
until I'm transposed
on the bar
room of a limousine.

Glory, or as near
as I know it,
has been reached
in these leather seats,

the codeine drip
of women's fingers
withdrawn
to slow my speech.

Let's open the sunroof.
Let's climb
through its tinted eye
and parachute

into the morass off
highway 16.
The locals will serve
us drinks.

When I'm alone I bask
in serotonin's
magnanimity,
the one-hundred-fifty

milligrams native
to those who need
to feel less.
Less is like turning

away from the wind-
shield's poultice,
the highway
of tears turned away

from death. Inside
the limousine
everything is just
as you would picture it—

mirrored walls,
palm fronds,
a dance floor danced
on in indifference.

Get up! Who cares
if the driver
fish-tails
without warning us?

Systole, diastole,
Cristal over-
flowing
behind two-way glass.

Let's open another
bottle. Mix in
some Valium
until we're consumed

like shadows
in the shadow
of the driver-side
camera, stage-

hands readying
the dolly and boom
as we gape
from the sunroof.

The sunroof is
a window—you can
see where I broke
a passenger's nose

with a bat. Glory,
or as near as I know it,
is bloodshed
after an attack.

By the time we reach
Vanderhoof
our touch will
electrify the dead—

they dance for love
of perfect pitch,
the high
when fingers on

their necks constrict,
glorious
and free among
the night's witnesses.

When I'm alone I bask
in the elegance
of the body's honesty—
all those beautiful

women angled to let
me see everything.
Uploaded on touch
they pixelate,

obscure my reflection
in the LCD,
their bodies dumped
roadside before

they become women
again. They fill
the culverts
where I rubberneck,

move across
the screen like an exit
wound relative
to its bullet's entrance.

Goodbye Athena.
Goodbye Persephone.
Palm fronds
wave and wave

and leave me stiff,
air conditioned
mouths
pricking my flesh.

I'll flag before I take
another cap.
Downed, dreaming
the dead meshed

in blood and soot,
passing over
the Athabasca in search
of new chemistry.

Entering the under-
world we row and row,
destiny sustained
in repetition—eyes

turned up, quivering
where we're ferried
across with all
the beautiful

women who sing
in unbelievably
high registers
about love and loss.

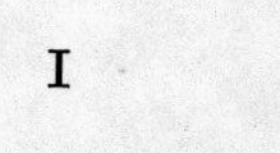

Vesica Piscis

Iron lung, the bifurcation of a scorpion's tail.
Viewed in thirds, venom extends

past the knuckle

on my father's ring finger,

spreads until it's closer than it appears. Why
won't he listen instead of repeating

this is pain and *this*

is pain and *this is pain?*

We hardly know each other, have never shown
weakness—not convinced of its existence

despite our privilege.

On second inspection,

it was a spider grazed him, legs lopped off
in the midst of a fit.

The only scorpions we've known

were kept as pets,

as minstrelsy, appendages that mimicked faces
beneath their masks.

Just as quickly as weakness

appears, it snaps back—

no breathing apparatus, no venom—only a victim
asking for a pill,

or *why aren't my pills*

where I left them?

If you think I'm ungrateful, try being betrayed
by the orthodoxy, your children,

and everyone else

who doubts the scorpion's malice.

After the fact.

The Lightning Field

If you see me, I can see you.
Hellbent on resistance,
the clearing where we move.
If you see me, I can see you
time ataxia's advance,
its many-tongued pursuit.
If you see me, I can see you—
upheld, hell-faced, seduced.

Labelled Faces in the Wild

Even waking is a kind of sleep,
consciousness standing
in for slow waves,
for start-to-start dependency.

In the wild, we're defenseless,
ones and zeros arrayed
in flux, on flood
plains where it's possible

to see beyond the quay.
Fever defines the perimeter.
Birds sucked into engines
and gorged by blades

of heat. Played back,
their clade recombines to form
Ophelia's data mask—
paint chipped, statistical,

sightline drained like air
space over the White House.
When the king wakes,
he wakes to ranks that close

like valves positioned
to bypass a stent, the cluster
of veins tied off
before a positive blood test.

As Conducted by Seiji Ozawa

Eight pm and an extended vowel
sounds from the pit, instruments
braying, sustaining the nasal
pitch of the audience. When
Massey Hall quiets, a spotlight sets
beyond its seats, and farther
back, porters place bets
on whether a gaffer will fall
from the rigging. My father
sits in the mezzanine. He practices
bruising his hand with his fist
as if he were damping a trombone—
in and out with mock innocence,
so like his son, getting it wrong.

Crane Fist

The sarcoma
the jaw's gape
the tether
its overreach

the interposed
the bed sheets
the bloody nose
its cartilage

the hail mary
the hangover
the bolus
its assayer

the leviathan
the grace note
the crane fist
its delayed blow

New Values

The fire was once a field.
The new world order

once the new world,
old gods tapping the glass

like drunks pausing
to feel the panes kick.

Here's a new one:
what do you call a man

who falls over while
unwrapping a lozenge?

Hypoglycemic.

The kind of parent
who'd set fire to a summer

drive, tell their kids
to *get out of the car*

and walk. When the curb
has overtaken the road,

those left join the traffic
that ran them aground.

I'd like to help, but I'm too
busy protecting myself.

II

Alprazolam

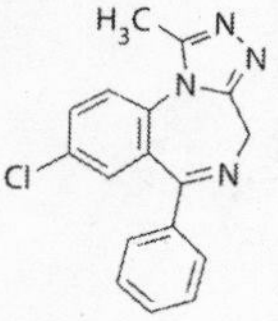

My first time, prone in the back
seat of a car. Skin horripilating
as if it had been kissed
and funnelled away in a storm,

aggregate of instinct and force
under pressure native
to a bomb. I try my muscles,
try harnessing the current

blunted by the road—
servant, mastered by departure—
opposite the new spine
expanding from the blacktop's

arc. Nothing. Around each
bend the continuum persists:
false horizon, second skin,
the meek inheriting the sins

of the well-heeled. What heals
once the threat ahead
has revealed its weaponry?
My last stand an inability

to stand up, stand my ground,
the route's hold less present
the more time we spend
together. Bound by gravity alone.

Something Like This But Not This

Hair of the dog.

Pixels compressed
into a demon
too great

to resist. Something
like muscle
memory,

the soul confirmed
by a slow
frame rate,

something
like a common
fish

fighting its reflection
in two-
way glass.

As if call and re-
call
were obsolete,

where and *when*
fused
into a premonition—

The Saint Tavern
after
too much drink.

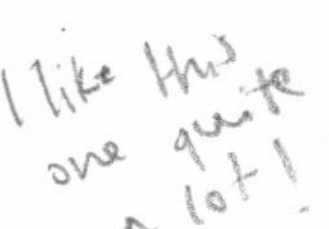

The Quick

Whoever is alone will stay alone.
After the quick and pointless
pleasure of being slapped,
the calm where hours stacked
on hours to become the future,
we could use a little luck:
a rising fever, a rabbit's foot
in Isobel's right pocket.
Barring that, we could chalk
outlines on the boardwalk,
lay low as we're drawn
and quartered in their Mondrian
frames. It's worthless to win
when winning is all you know.

Self-Portrait as Anything at Any Cost

Consumed by greed

even my family doesn't recognize me:
eyes set close,

prey squared up
in rays

unrolled like film from a long-distance

camera.

Developed, mania splits
the mind's roof,

the sclera where I swoop down

for a look,

swoop to feed on anything at any cost:
lost love,

the furnace made hot by another's

words,

square pupils stilled
until the seas part

part and parcel with what I've become.

Parasite. Threadworm.

Treacle
laced tentacles licking the dirt.

It's plain I'm desperate,

slaver for more,
slobber to appear everywhere—

hail helmeting the world

elementally.

Each time I exhale
I unlearn land, sea, and air,

the sword iris
thrashing

the heath until gluttonous guts spill

and consequence,
always dependable,

stoops

like a body bent over its walking stick—

done to a turn, done too
soon,

done to death.

Meditation

after Charles Baudelaire

Come down. Let's reclaim
the night's straight-
edged stutter, the decline
that coffins the city's

alleyways where we cut
ourselves for peace,
for pleasure. Let's meet
at the border, unseen

from balconies that open
on the sea, the harbour,

our prototypes defenseless
against the water's
blur of waking eyes,
the reminder that we're sober.

Venlafaxine

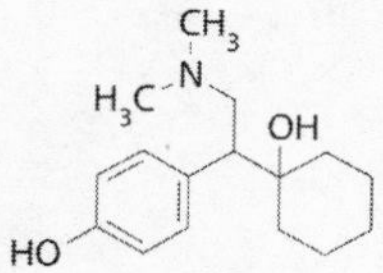

The needle dropped out of habit,
tongue interlocking with a tooth
cut groove. On Roncesvalles,
before command reinforced
our fear of shame, we'd circle
Sorauren Avenue Park like wolves
loosed from the infirmary.
The dame's rockets were armed
with blossoms, and because
we were free to fill in the field's
texture, its grass and grain,
I'd slide disks from poly sleeves
as my brother cased the corner
where moths lined the gates
like lookouts beating
through an unchanged city.
Before the caps downed to keep
us *more us*, the gates were
peacock blue. The blues rerun,
each note held where an ocean
threatened to overthrow the stylus
mid-song, tidal flats diminishing
our senses, our sense of self.
Painted with a too small hand,
you can see how brush strokes
overwhelm the mind, the cortex
questioning *are we not? Are
we not more than the first word
or the last?* Whoever set

our interrogation to consciousness
set it on the LP we mistook
for landscape, set it with recurring
strain, dizziness overwhelming
the park's round. Curfew.
Tonight I'll move over shared
ground: my mind free to feel,
free will rippling out like shark gills.

yoooooo

III

Spirits of the Grotto

Luis Jacob, 2012

Heels on gravel, and further off
a siren that hasn't lulled in hours,
the underpass where streetlights
circle like low-level drones.
I pass the facade with my wife,
the two of us alone with thirty
sets of eyes: owl and avatar,
moth wing and mirror ball
following an ambulance over
Dufferin Gate Bridge. When
its spell subsides we come
across a shoe and the shoe fits—
our ghosts a series of mistimed steps,
the grotto scaled, foot by foot.

Carisoprodol

When someone asks you to keep a secret,
that secret is a lie.

Pink powder crushed
into a dial

tone, the neon sign
dissolving

a motel window's latent high.

At the Grand
every room has an ocean-side view.

Barrel curls drumming.

On the eve of the grand opening
a guest knifed

into the pink light
of the swimming pool,

forgetting her initial pause,

the fluorescent buds
of her fresh tattoo.

Forgetting that consciousness wades in
at high tide

before passing through—

The Lightning Field (2)

Fire discolours the field
like a rabbit smothered
in the crosshairs
of a rifle—stray, primal,
vanishing point
extended by the emerging
sun. Strike anywhere
and invite resurrection.

Kindness

Been there, done that.
Senses multiplied
like accordion bellows,
the earth laid flat.

Stepping from its lip
I begin to feel my body
equalize as I smoke,
my crew cut a jet stream

when the drugs kick in—
synapses dimmed
like gold rings bubbling
in glasses of champagne.

It's summer, cicadas
hissing beyond the yard
where I cross
myself with the mobile's

receiver when it rings.
I've known so much
kindness it's hard
to recognize the real thing.

About Face

I can't tell a sliver from a seed.
I can't tell a fever from its peak.

I can't tell words from an attack.
But I can tell you that you can't.

I can't tell over from overuse.
I can't tell 'no' from an excuse.

I can't tell timing from bad luck.
But I can tell you that you can't.

I can't tell flags from opera blood.
I can't tell outrage from WTF.

I can't tell forever to fall back.
But I can tell you that you can't.

Varadero

Sinking into the reef
a sail divides
surf from the 'v'

burnt on your chest:
coral, blood-
leaf, the difference

between the cliff-
face that chips
away like slate

and the half hitch
where the equator
finds its shape.

On a shared path
we pedal
along the beach,

waves advancing,
arriving
at our full height.

*

Bloodleaf—sure as
time is
a circle that repeats,

appears briefly
as a nautilus
turning back to

exchange its shell,
allowing
us to see each

other on opposing
shores,
opposing wills.

IV

Ovid, *Metamorphoses* XIV, 223-319

I.

I came to next to the guesthouse,
Alex handing me a copy
of *Modern Man* as we took in
the first nude we'd ever
seen. The pages stuttered:
identical bodies distinguished
by setting, pose, the fingers
of boys whorled in Circe's
ink-smeared anatomy—
sacred heart, vasculature—
Alex and I transfixed,
sitting stock-still as she bled out.

2.

Without clothes we were different.
Offset at the waist, Circe's skin
fixed in laminate, cuffed, cold,
more animal than our classmates
standing ten-fingered and ten-
toed like unwanted dogs. They
crouched, cannibals masking
the stoop with pictures of women
who resembled Saints
we were told could save us
as we turned towards new idols.
Their hair crowning like waterfalls.

3.

I asked: *Let the sun burn my eyes,*
let it burn my back. If change
were to come, it would come
unnoticed, reddening my sight
as smoke filled the parking lot
behind the quarry. Now
fourteen, weed demon inhaling
the sky, I hungered for oblivion
before I knew it as an island
of housing tracts that concealed
the dead, afternoons spent
crossing in and out of sedition.

e—restraint sapped
nal spell. Why not
get high? Hash on hot knives,
acid's bristling tongue wagging
where my friends surrendered
to mutation: long snouts, the hair
of swine, war paint bulging
over wine-stained hides. Two
tabs and I'd eat my entire family,
the twig and berry coverings
that defined our colony. Free-
basing, bottomed out in a trough.

5.

Seen from a distance, each trip
came on like fever; injury
and infection, their blessings
limiting our capacity to alter
the future. Tending to the ill,
only Alex was left to witness
the retreat of the dragon's tail,
the blast and spray of need
foaming in the corners
of its mouth, our mouths,
brothers and sisters in the word
and the word no more than hunger.

6.

And when change came, it came
with a crossbow's bolt,
Alex on the corner throwing
shade, a quiver of police
pulled from an unmarked
van. He ran—a hundred tabs
of LSD jammed against
the hyperbaric chamber
of his chest—and later, in custody,
down the front of his pants.
Dealers, defenders, friends—
we were blotted by his sacred hand.

7.

He asked: *Let it sear through*
my tights, I'll feel wide open.
Alone, twitching while a flash-
light was held to the dark
of his face. He'd hear us laugh,
call out, our true bodies
restored, replaying the first
image he'd known—Circe:
regal, flowering, spread-eagled
where they'd wed. She hovered,
the remains of the day receding,
leashed to the head of a bird.

8.

Some hallucinations are stronger
than others: the blue of five-
dollar bills become water,
become waves, powder rimming
the paper's edge like salt
seasoning a glass. When we've
finished inhaling we'll print
more. When we've finished
inhaling, our money will bear
the face of the new king—nettles
and flame extending from his brow,
Alex grinning in a fast food crown.

V

The Saint Tavern

We last until last call—strobe
boxing our ears, patrons
praying to the patron saint
of *when*? Inside, one of us
wanted to know how it felt
to unclasp the pendant
decorating my wife's neck,
the flipbook flipped
to confirm our presence.
It's face alive. It's face her own—
a spear and its principle
of balance, chronometer
counting down to a new age.
There I dream she's no longer
my wife; the tavern's
rafters warped into a fortress,
the sucker-punch of a see-
through dress clinging
just long enough to deceive.
Look, you can see it gather
as she steps from clay,
spear thrust half-way
into the next-in-line to buy a drink.

Future Shock

The mob means well.

Like the time a Virginia
gunman mistook
his firearm for a camera:

precision achieved
in the manner of the un-
manned, the portal

where we stormed news
stations on tablets
to commandeer the future.

Avenue of eyes.

Avenue of onlookers
panting in the road,
adopting the breathless

hunted feeling
of animals scattered
from their packs,

a single shooter
and the horde's
collective crush. Our fear.

The Lightning Field (3)

Our heads meet where current
lowers into a crown.
The sky is clear, its accent
sustained in the crowd
partitioned single file
on the park's cortical grid—
onlookers immobilized,
present and past recurrent, wed.

Elegy for Lincoln Beachey

$L - \frac{1}{2} p v^2 \, A C_L$

When air becomes fuel,
it's all we can do
to hold back tomorrow—

past twelve, flares light
the bay where rainfall
is prepared for extended

release. Then silence.
Canopus 13 above
the Panama-Pacific

exhibition lacing the air
with exhaust that rolls in
like the head of state

unveiled as death.
His presence darkens
the Honeymoon Bridge—

what is and what is not
converging the way
contrails imitate type,

the sky plunging
from a paradise of flags
that spell *Good Night.*

The same words written
by Art Smith when
he takes flight, global

positioning abandoned
for the hype of a vertical
drop. Our kingdom

for a last resort.
Our kingdom
for the commander-in-chief.

The Last Will Be First

It's not enough
    to bind
your arm with a belt.
    The sky

is creased, holds
    fast where
your body wills
    each knot's

refusal. One day
    your hands
are letters, the next
    they bell

like leather trained
    to give
beneath a blow.
    Hold still

while the heavy
    bag ropes
the floor in shadow,
    cuckolds

the first responder
    assembled
imperfectly
    in its lasso.

Lip Service

Speak of the Devil, the Devil
appears: a beast with two
backs, the not-meant-to-be
revealed in the headlights
of a passing car. Fire is
my shepherd; I shall not
want. I lie down in green
pastures until my heart stops.

Underneath my wife it's summer.
A bed of pine needles covering
the forest floor. Underneath
my wife I thrust until her lips
are the pursed picture
of happiness. When we adopt
a single sex, summer blooms
like a liar in the middle of a lie.

In the twentieth century I can
never die. '78, '87, '95—
the tipping point tripped
where time divides—
we'll survive its draw
and pivot, days re-created
in the future's image—
before we go our separate ways.

And earlier, Vlad Tepes' curls
curled from a block of wood—
hipster chic. Waxed mustache,
blushing cheek. His internal
monologue a flood of ink
fixed to what remains
of his cognomen, a stamped
face that continues to speak.

We suspend our disbelief,
yet continue to fall in love
with everything we make.
The thread that holds
the underworld in place,
the mosaic of buildings
built on such a scale
that to look down is to feel sick.

Look down: the ground
repeats hundreds of times
before its miniaturization
dissimilates—the city's
dysplasia shuttered
with the raised skirts
of reflective tents. Don't
just stand there, run for cover.

Run past the lift hauled
by the surface-to-air
recovery system,
past lovers lip-locked
with the sense of someone
listening, someone trying
to decipher an accent,
tongue divorced from web.

To communicate speak
into the voice user
interface. I read my will
and am told that will
won't determine my fate.
In everything there's order.
In everything
there's a second state.

When the Black Bloc arrives,
separate but equal sirens
call from a sea of acetylene.
Judge not lest ye be armed;
masked in scarves
and sunglasses
while a wave of bodies destroys
what continues to regenerate.

Anger. Sunlight. The words
I've scribbled out
then written again
like conversation replayed
on a black box.
Don't ask about survivors.
Don't ask why everything
is happening at once.

My favourite photograph: a man
falling from the World Trade
Center like a champagne cork
flooding the sky. Last seen
at 9:41 am, north tower.
Hello. We're overlooking
the Financial Center.
Three of us. Two broken windows.

The living can't help but defy
the dead. When the pilot
turns, the horizon multiplies
behind his head: a meadow
of cloud, the past
sliding past a passenger-
side window like a shark
nosing towards someone else.

I'll keep going until you make
me stop. I'm the kind of man
who expects you to remember
his name, who'll talk over you
when you talk. Given
the chance to do evil, I've done
so—traded a moment's death
to rise again tomorrow.

Underneath my wife it rains.
Repeat after me: do you take
the end of the world, the shelter
of its black wings, to have
and to hold, in sickness
and in health, like money
passed among the millionfold,
so help you God?

I do.

The end of beauty is rooted
in inertia, the interchange-
ability of place. Repeat
after me: the less I have
to lose the closer I come
to being untouchable. Vlad
the Impaler carved before
the bread and wine at his table.

In everything there's order.
First fire, then its point
of ignition—the spectre
of the *Y* that defies sin.
Forgive me my trespass
as I forgive the bodies
that bubble and set,
natureless and animate.

Bodies rigged like wind
ignored on a runway.
Light-years measured
in electric light.
What a medium passes off
as sleight of hand: the ability
to return to the world
as it was originally found.

I'll keep going until I
can't help myself. A last
moment of lucidity
before my voice emulates
tape hiss. The last
time I'll do something
awful to prevent
myself from doing worse.

hard.

Let the record show
the beast with two backs
has been domesticated.
We suspend our disbelief
as cells are coupled
with glass, mounted
beneath an eye that guides
their recurring motifs.

This service is for lovers
who've fallen behind.
The withered field
that holds us at its highest
point, unconscious,
while summer declines.
The grass that climbs
and thickens into a tongue.

This service is for lovers
who still believe. Repeat
after me: a third leg
will be buried in my un-
marked grave. As for my
own identity, the 'Johnstone'
coat of arms is tattooed
between my shoulder blades.

NOTES

"The Chemical Life" incorporates quotes from a Billy Corgan interview published in *Stereogum* on August 19, 2014.

"Labelled Faces in the Wild" is titled after a database of photographs designed for studying unconstrained facial recognition.

"The Quick" was written in response to Ian Williams's "After Autumn".

"Ovid, *Metamorphoses* XIV, 223-319" incorporates lyrics from the Wavves song "King of the Beach."

"Elegy for Lincoln Beachey" is prefaced by the equation that measures an aircraft's lift during known flow conditions.

ACKNOWLEDGMENTS

My thanks to the editors of the following publications where poems in *The Chemical Life* previously appeared:

Ambit (UK): "Carisoprodol", "Venlafaxine"
The Antigonish Review: "The Last Will Be First"
Arc Poetry Magazine: "The Chemical Life", "The Saint Tavern"
The Fiddlehead: "Elegy for Lincoln Beachey", "Future Shock", "Vesica Piscis"
Fjords (US): "Spirits of the Grotto"
Grain: "Lip Service"
Island (AU): "Alprazolam"
Maisonneuve: "Ovid, *Metamorphoses* XIV, 223-319"
The Malahat Review: "Labelled Faces in the Wild"
North American Review (US): "Kindness"
Taddle Creek: "New Values"
This Magazine: "Crane Fist", "Something Like This But Not This"
The Walrus: "As Conducted by Seiji Ozawa"

"The Quick" was anthologized in *Tag: Canadian Poets at Play*.

"The Lightning Field (2)" was featured in the "Post Me a Card" exhibit at the Red Head Gallery in July 2017.

My thanks to the Canada Council of the Arts, the Ontario Arts Council and the Toronto Arts Council for funding that sustained me while writing this book.

ALSO BY JIM JOHNSTONE

Poetry

The Velocity of Escape (2008)
Patternicity (2010)
Sunday, the locusts (2011)
Dog Ear (2014)
The Chemical Life (2017)

Chapbooks

Siamese Poems (2006)
Epoch (2013)
Microaggressions (2016)

Criticism

The Essential Earle Birney (2014)
The Essential D. G. Jones (2016)

Carmine Starnino, Editor
Michael Harris, Founding Editor

SELECTED POEMS David Solway
THE MULBERRY MEN David Solway
A SLOW LIGHT Ross Leckie
NIGHT LETTERS Bill Furey
COMPLICITY Susan Glickman
A NUN'S DIARY Ann Diamond
CAVALIER IN A ROUNDHEAD SCHOOL Errol MacDonald
VEILED COUNTRIES/LIVES Marie-Claire Blais (Translated by Michael Harris)
BLIND PAINTING Robert Melançon (Translated by Philip Stratford)
SMALL HORSES & INTIMATE BEASTS Michel Garneau
(Translated by Robert McGee)
IN TRANSIT Michael Harris
THE FABULOUS DISGUISE OF OURSELVES Jan Conn
ASHBOURN John Reibetanz
THE POWER TO MOVE Susan Glickman
MAGELLAN'S CLOUDS Robert Allen
MODERN MARRIAGE David Solway
K. IN LOVE Don Coles
THE INVISIBLE MOON Carla Hartsfield
ALONG THE ROAD FROM EDEN George Ellenbogen
DUNINO Stephen Scobie
KINETIC MUSTACHE Arthur Clark
RUE SAINTE FAMILLE Charlotte Hussey
HENRY MOORE'S SHEEP Susan Glickman
SOUTH OF THE TUDO BEM CAFÉ Jan Conn
THE INVENTION OF HONEY Ricardo Sternberg
EVENINGS AT LOOSE ENDS Gérald Godin (Translated by Judith Cowan)
THE PROVING GROUNDS Rhea Tregebov
LITTLE BIRD Don Coles
HOMETOWN Laura Lush
FORTRESS OF CHAIRS Elisabeth Harvor
NEW & SELECTED POEMS Michael Harris
BEDROCK David Solway
TERRORIST LETTERS Ann Diamond
THE SIGNAL ANTHOLOGY Edited by Michael Harris
MURMUR OF THE STARS: SELECTED SHORTER POEMS Peter Dale Scott
WHAT DANTE DID WITH LOSS Jan Conn
MORNING WATCH John Reibetanz
JOY IS NOT MY PROFESSION Muhammad al-Maghut
(Translated by John Asfour and Alison Burch)
WRESTLING WITH ANGELS: SELECTED POEMS Doug Beardsley
HIDE & SEEK Susan Glickman
MAPPING THE CHAOS Rhea Tregebov
FIRE NEVER SLEEPS Carla Hartsfield
THE RHINO GATE POEMS George Ellenbogen
SHADOW CABINET Richard Sanger
MAP OF DREAMS Ricardo Sternberg
THE NEW WORLD Carmine Starnino
THE LONG COLD GREEN EVENINGS OF SPRING Elisabeth Harvor
KEEP IT ALL Yves Boisvert (Translated by Judith Cowan)

THE GREEN ALEMBIC Louise Fabiani
THE ISLAND IN WINTER Terence Young
A TINKERS' PICNIC Peter Richardson
SARACEN ISLAND: THE POEMS OF ANDREAS KARAVIS David Solway
BEAUTIES ON MAD RIVER: SELECTED AND NEW POEMS Jan Conn
WIND AND ROOT Brent MacLaine
HISTORIES Andrew Steinmetz
ARABY Eric Ormsby
WORDS THAT WALK IN THE NIGHT Pierre Morency
(Translated by Lissa Cowan and René Brisebois)
A PICNIC ON ICE: SELECTED POEMS Matthew Sweeney
HELIX: NEW AND SELECTED POEMS John Steffler
HERESIES: THE COMPLETE POEMS OF ANNE WILKINSON, 1924-1961
Edited by Dean Irvine
CALLING HOME Richard Sanger
FIELDER'S CHOICE Elise Partridge
MERRYBEGOT Mary Dalton
MOUNTAIN TEA Peter Van Toorn
AN ABC OF BELLY WORK Peter Richardson
RUNNING IN PROSPECT CEMETERY Susan Glickman
MIRABEL Pierre Nepveu (Translated by Judith Cowan)
POSTSCRIPT Geoffrey Cook
STANDING WAVE Robert Allen
THERE, THERE Patrick Warner
HOW WE ALL SWIFTLY: THE FIRST SIX BOOKS Don Coles
THE NEW CANON: AN ANTHOLOGY OF CANADIAN POETRY
Edited by Carmine Starnino
OUT TO DRY IN CAPE BRETON Anita Lahey
RED LEDGER Mary Dalton
REACHING FOR CLEAR David Solway
OX Christopher Patton
THE MECHANICAL BIRD Asa Boxer
SYMPATHY FOR THE COURIERS Peter Richardson
MORNING GOTHIC: NEW AND SELECTED POEMS George Ellenbogen
36 CORNELIAN AVENUE Christopher Wiseman
THE EMPIRE'S MISSING LINKS Walid Bitar
PENNY DREADFUL Shannon Stewart
THE STREAM EXPOSED WITH ALL ITS STONES D.G. Jones
PURE PRODUCT Jason Guriel
ANIMALS OF MY OWN KIND Harry Thurston
BOXING THE COMPASS Richard Greene
CIRCUS Michael Harris
THE CROW'S VOW Susan Briscoe
WHERE WE MIGHT HAVE BEEN Don Coles
MERIDIAN LINE Paul Bélanger (Translated by Judith Cowan)
SKULLDUGGERY Asa Boxer
SPINNING SIDE KICK Anita Lahey
THE ID KID Linda Besner
GIFT HORSE Mark Callanan
SUMPTUARY LAWS Nyla Matuk
THE GOLDEN BOOK OF BOVINITIES Robert Moore
MAJOR VERBS Pierre Nepveu (Translated by Donald Winkler)
ALL SOULS' Rhea Tregebov
THE SMOOTH YARROW Susan Glickman
THE GREY TOTE Deena Kara Shaffer
HOOKING Mary Dalton

DANTE'S HOUSE Richard Greene
BIRDS FLOCK FISH SCHOOL Edward Carson
SATISFYING CLICKING SOUND Jason Guriel
DOG EAR Jim Johnstone
THE SCARBOROUGH Michael Lista
RADIO WEATHER Shoshanna Wingate
LAWS & LOCKS Chad Campbell
LEAVING THE ISLAND Talya Rubin
INSTALLATIONS David Solway
MOCKINGBIRD Derek Webster
LATE VICTORIANS Vincent Colistro
MODEL DISCIPLE Michael Prior
BASED ON ACTUAL EVENTS Robert Moore
STRANGER Nyla Matuk
SIREN Kateri Lanthier
TABLE MANNERS Catriona Wright
SHIP OF GOLD: THE ESSENTIAL POEMS OF ÉMILE NELLIGAN (Trans. by Marc di Saverio)
THE CHEMICAL LIFE Jim Johnstone